# Do It
# for
# Yourself

A
MOTIVATIONAL
JOURNAL

by Kara Cutruzzula
illustrated by Tessa Forrest

ABRAMS IMAGE, NEW YORK

# Introduction

**Motivation.**

**Want more of it?**

**Of course you do.**

Motivation is the not-so-secret sauce to getting closer to what you want. Sure, you can dream and plan and plot, but without the motivation to see a goal through, all of your wild ambitions can feel stalled—or worse, like they're nowhere to be found.

You need motivation to blow past the roadblocks that arrive in every shape, size, and form. These barriers can halt a new project before it even gets off the ground. Maybe your roadblock is internal, like a negative voice that pops up in your head every time you attempt something new. Maybe your block is tied to envy, and you're intimidated by other people achieving goals that look just like yours. Or maybe your block shows up because you feel powerless—like there's never enough time, energy, or money to stay on track.

All of these blocks are valid (and valuable) signals. And rather than pretending they don't exist, you can harness tools that will help you understand and untangle every one. I trust that these tools work because I've used them myself, and they helped me develop from an insecure and indecisive writer who loved to procrastinate into one who's no longer afraid of sharing her work and reaching for the biggest possible dreams.

The process starts by finding out what motivates *you*—not your coworker, your neighbor, or the valedictorian of your high school class. Once you get going, you will learn how to build momentum, push past hurdles, finish what you started, and look to the future.

You're seeking change. Perhaps you're switching careers. Or embarking on a challenging work or creative project. Or you simply want to explore new ideas that make you feel less bored and more alive every single day.

Whatever your goal, isn't it time to get inspired?

Welcome to your guide for starting, finishing, and—most of all—*doing* it for yourself.

**Let's begin.**

# CHAPTER 01

# Getting Going

## What do you want?

This is one of those questions that fall under the "simple to ask, tricky to answer" category. Clearly, you want to find the motivation for *something*. So what is that big, shiny thing? Is it something related to your career? Your personal life? A hobby you're about to begin?

Think about it. Hold it in your mind. Say it out loud: I want _____.
*(Nobody's watching you, I promise.)*

Now, here is the all-important follow-up: Why? Why do you want it? Do you want to make more money? Do you want a sense of fulfillment? Do you want to quit your day job? Your reason should be as personal and specific as possible. Maybe you want to stretch your abilities, become self-sufficient, shake up your routine, or prove something to yourself.

Your *why* is crucial—it's the thread tying you to your future. Take a moment now to pick your target. This is a relaxed time, full of freedom, of preparing and percolating. Then, use the following exercises to help create the spark to light you up and go after it.

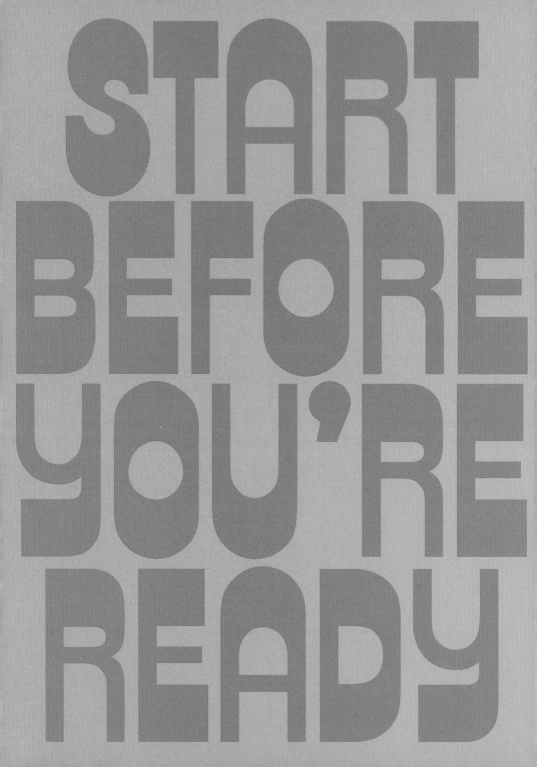

Is fear holding
you back from
beginning?

Fear is often tied to the perceived impossibility of an end goal, one that's too overwhelming to believe you can accomplish. So let's not think about the end just yet. Let's consider the present.

**What is the tiniest step you can take to start? Write it down here—and give yourself a deadline for when it will be done.**

See? You're starting.

**Step 1:**

Fiancial Freedom
Part Time Job
Companion

**Deadline:**

Now

Creating an anchor, mantra, or mission statement to come back to can keep you calm and focused.

Instead of thinking about what you want, act as if you have already achieved it. Instead of saying *I want* (as in *I want to be a writer* or *I want to run my own business*) change the thought to *I am* (*I am a writer* and *I am an entrepreneur*).

Write your new anchor here ten times and say it to yourself at set points throughout the day. (Right when you wake up is a good time.)

1. Debt Free
2. Debt Free
3. Debt Free
4. Debt Free
5. Debt Free
6. Debt Free
7. Debt Free
8. Debt Free
9. Debt Free
10. Debt Free

Creating a vision
board can help you
gain clarity on the
people, places, and
things you want in
your world.

**So let's make a vision board, but with words. Cover this page with phrases that represent the life you want to lead.**

# We all have hidden talents. What is one thing you suspect you might be good at, but have never tried?

**Share that thing here and explain why you haven't tried it yet.**

# What (or who) supports the pursuit of your project?

Maybe your day job gives you flexibility and income, or a significant other is providing emotional encouragement.

**Acknowledge everything you are grateful for now, as you start this process.**

GRATEFUL
THANKFUL
GRATEFUL
THANKFUL
GRATEFUL
THANKFUL
GRATEFUL
THANKFUL
GRATEFUL

You don't have to wait to see what lies ahead, you can plan it now.

**Write your own Wikipedia entry from the future: Detail what's already happened, and go far into what's to come, spanning your entire life and career.**

Dream big, and think about how your current project connects to that dream. How will it help get you there?

Challenges spring up at the start of any project, but many of them come from overactive imaginations.

Our brains predict what *might* be difficult. So beat your brain to it.

**Make a bulleted list of everything that *could* be a problem. Then add a star next to every item that doesn't have a solution. You might be surprised by what you find.**

- _____

- _____

- _____

- _____

- _____

- _____

- _____

- _____

- _____

- _____

DON'T MISS
OUT ON
SOME
THING THAT
COULD BE
GREAT JUST
BECAUSE IT
COULD ALSO
BE DIFFICULT.

# Name three notable people you admire.

They should be your heroes in some way.

Now consider your own skills and interests. In what ways do you overlap with these people? Perhaps you have the same sense of style, the same level of ambition, or a similar background.

**Find one trait that connects you with each hero.**

See, you have more in common with greatness than you realize.

**Name:**

_____

**Trait:**

_____

**Name:**

_____

**Trait:**

_____

**Name:**

_____

**Trait:**

_____

## Jealousy is a major enemy of creativity.

Don't let this energy-sucking monster hurt your progress.

It's time to get it all out. **Write down everything and everyone who inspires envy** in you and leave them all on the page.

# What's itching your brain right now?

Do you keep thinking about returning to your photography practice, following up with a friend who offered to read your work, or learning a new language?

These itches are gut feelings that only grow more persistent with time.

**Let's chronicle yours: When did you first get the itch? Try to recall the specific time, date, or event. How often have you thought about it since?**

GUT
FEELIN—
GS    ARE
GUARD—
IAN
ANGELS

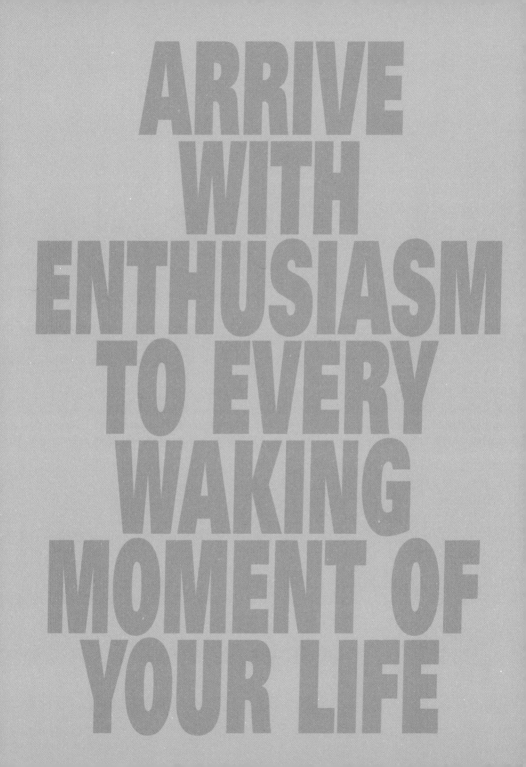

# When was the last time you bounded out of bed, excited for your day?

Get very specific about what gave you that energy: an important meeting, a fresh idea, an imminent deadline?

**How can you re-create that feeling today?**

There are millions of people out in the world racking up accomplishments. But you can choose whether they inspire you—or make you envious.

**Instead of wasting time thinking about a nemesis who has everything you want, write a fan letter to someone you admire.**

And when you're finished, consider reaching out.

Dear _____

_____

_____

_____

_____

_____

_____

_____

_____

_____

_____

_____

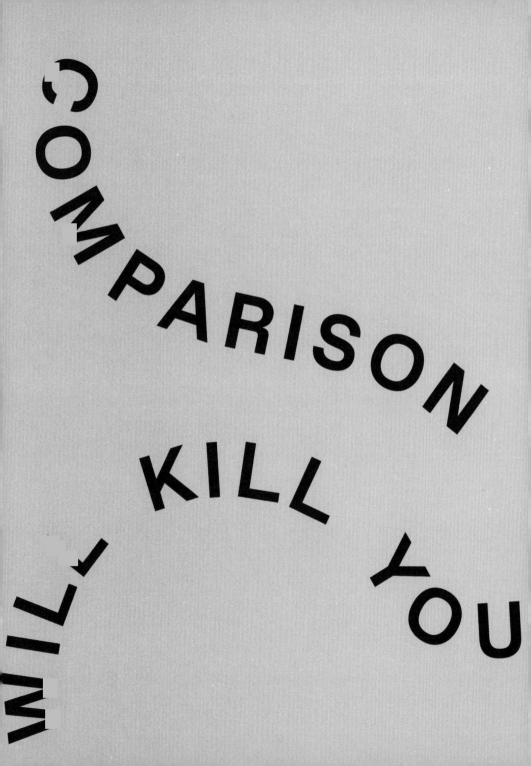

There are an incredible 1,440 minutes in a day.

Many of your minutes are already accounted for, but if you can find even a few extra ones, they can help chip away at your goal. I believe you can.

**Where can you find some time to spare? Can you commit ten minutes to your project today? Or even five?**

**How will you use those minutes?**

Decision fatigue is real. There's a giant benefit to finding a few choices you can simplify.

Maybe you can embrace a uniform at work so you don't have to debate your outfit as often. Or you can eat the same breakfast to minimize decision-making.

**Name three tasks you feel slow you down every morning, then try to come up with one solution for each of them.**

**Task #1:**

_____

**Solution:**

_____

**Task #2:**

_____

**Solution:**

_____

**Task #3:**

_____

**Solution:**

_____

No book originates as a *New York Times* bestseller, and no revolutionary business is founded overnight.

You never see anyone's first attempt (and no one has to see yours). So what's there to lose?

**Begin a first draft here of anything you wish.**

# CHAPTER 02

# Building Momentum

## Where are you now?

Maybe you're having a really productive day—or a productive week—and you're dominating your work, getting everything done, somehow even juggling last-minute errands. But it can feel impossible to run at the same pace forever. How can you keep this up and not get caught in a slump?

Or perhaps you're at the beginning stages of what feels like a good routine, and you don't want to mess anything up. How can you continue your progress and not flame out?

These feelings are understandable. You want to grab on tightly to what's working and leave the rest behind. How do you do it? Here's a clue: The ability to maintain your enthusiasm for a new project or practice usually comes from a carefully executed plan.

You can structure your momentum by giving yourself boundaries, progress reports, and check-ins. The following tools will help clarify your ideas, develop positive routines, and cultivate even more anticipation and excitement for your future.

It's time to seize what lies ahead.

# Why do some good days feel effortless?

They don't happen by magic—which means you can make them happen more often.

**Make a list of all the activities that would occur during your ideal day of working and creating, whether that's brainstorming, collaborating, reading, or something else.**

**Then, circle the actions you have control over.**

You now have a recipe for re-creating your ideal day.

- _____
- _____
- _____
- _____
- _____
- _____
- _____
- _____
- _____
- _____

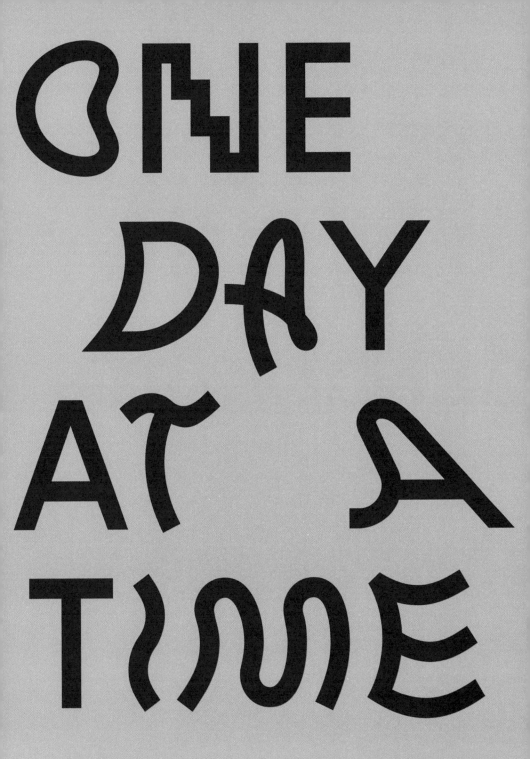

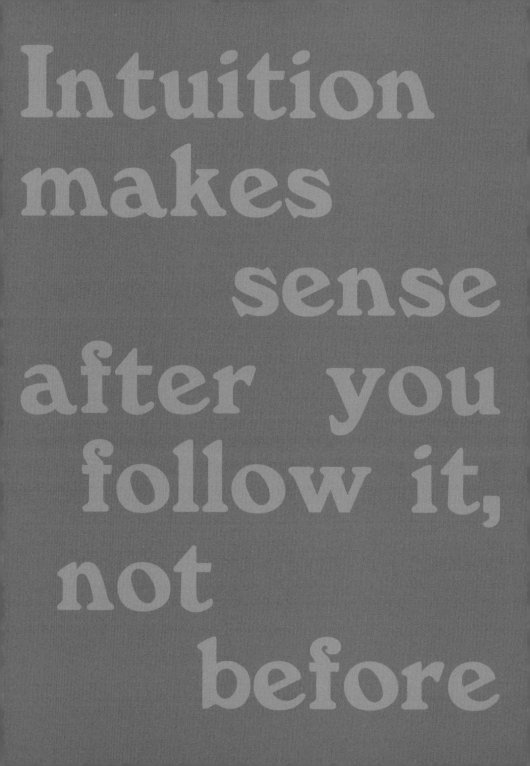

Intuition
makes
sense
after you
follow it,
not
before

# Are you ignoring your intuition?

Think of an occasion where you paid close attention to that little voice that told you "go left" when the rest of the world was saying "go right." What happened? Now think of another occasion where you didn't listen to that voice: What happened then?

**Get very quiet—and honest. What is your intuition telling you about your project right now?**

Every day, we try to minimize risk—it's easier to not do something hard. Yet that mind-set can keep us living small lives.

To expand, you must leap. And to leap, you must start by asking for help.

**What do you need right now? Advice? An extra pair of eyes? A mentor?**

Think of someone who might be able to help, and ask that person for a small favor today.

LEAP AND
THE NET
WILL
APPEAR

# Are you a compliment acceptor or a compliment deflector?

An acceptor gratefully takes positive feedback with a simple "Thank you," while a deflector might respond with little jabs of self-criticism: "I had a lot of help" or "Oh, you don't really mean that."

**What is the last compliment you received? Recall the details and share whether you believe the praise to be true.**

You deserve success. You deserve happiness. You deserve love. You deserve a life lived in Technicolor, filled with everything you can imagine.

That's what I think you deserve. **What do you think you deserve?**

**I deserve:**

_____

_____

_____

_____

_____

_____

_____

_____

_____

_____

_____

Every email or
tweet you send,
every hi to a
stranger or "Hey,
love your work!"
is the seed of a
future opportunity.

You don't know which ones will
grow, so you simply have to
plant them all. And then wait.

**Which seeds will you deploy
today?**

# THE DAY
# YOU PLANT
# THE SEED
# IS NOT
# THE DAY
# YOU EAT
# THE FRUIT

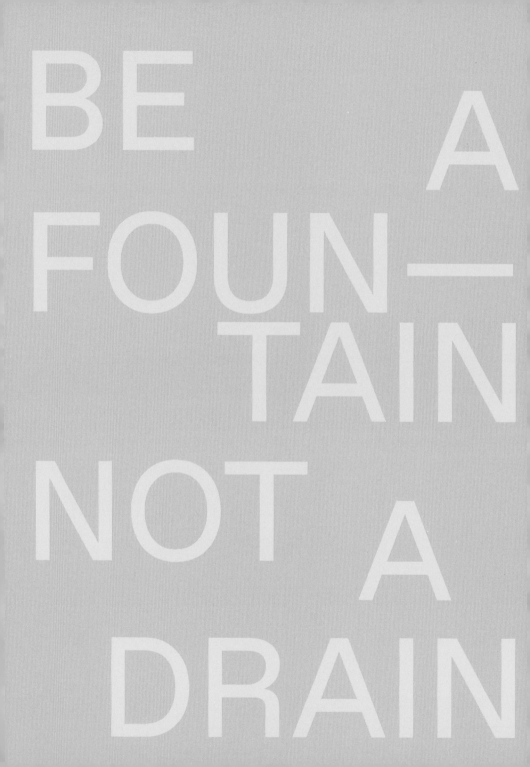

You absorb the emotions and energies of people around you, whether you want to or not.

If you're surrounded by people who suck up energy (the drains), you might become a drainer, too. But when you're near energy-giving people (the fountains), you begin to give more.

**Name the three most positive people you know.** Think of ways to spend more time with them, whether by setting up a coffee date, kickstarting a new project together, or just talking more often to bask in their good energy.

1. _____

_____

_____

2. _____

_____

_____

3. _____

_____

_____

# Can you feel it?

That all-encompassing *it* contains the success you're seeking, the finish line you can barely see, and the drive to get you there. It's the complete and unwavering belief that you are going to make it, no matter what.

Can you feel it?

**Reveal what it feels like here.**

What if your main
goal wasn't to finish
or to just get by—
what if your main
goal was excellence?

**Describe what a day of
striving for excellence would
look like for you.**

What's the first thing you would do in the **morning**?

_____

_____

_____

How can you push yourself during one **midday** task?

_____

_____

_____

Finally, what **nighttime** ritual would set up tomorrow for
excellence, too?

_____

_____

_____

# Do you need more time?

Think you can spare a moment for what I call One Creative Minute?

**Grab your phone or look at the clock, and set a timer for a single, solitary minute. When the timer starts ticking, make something—anything—in this space.**

Don't stop until the minute is up. Then look at what you've done.

# THINGS
# OF
# QUALITY
# HAVE NO
# FEAR
# OF TIME

I relax

I let go

my life          is

in          perfect

flow

A state of flow arrives when you're working at the edge of your capabilities— you're paddling, but haven't waded into the deep end. Time seems to stop altogether.

**When is the last time you experienced flow? What were you doing? List everything out here.** (Essential ingredients for me are a looming deadline, a challenging task, and the absence of distractions.)

Can you give yourself the space—and ingredients—to find your flow again?

- _____
- _____
- _____
- _____
- _____
- _____
- _____
- _____
- _____
- _____

# Who always sees you in a positive light?

Is it a grandparent, teacher, sibling, or close friend? Their beliefs about you are probably more accurate than your own—it's difficult to see our own strengths, so use this person as a mirror.

What qualities do you think they see in you? **Write down all the words you believe they would use to describe you to a stranger.**

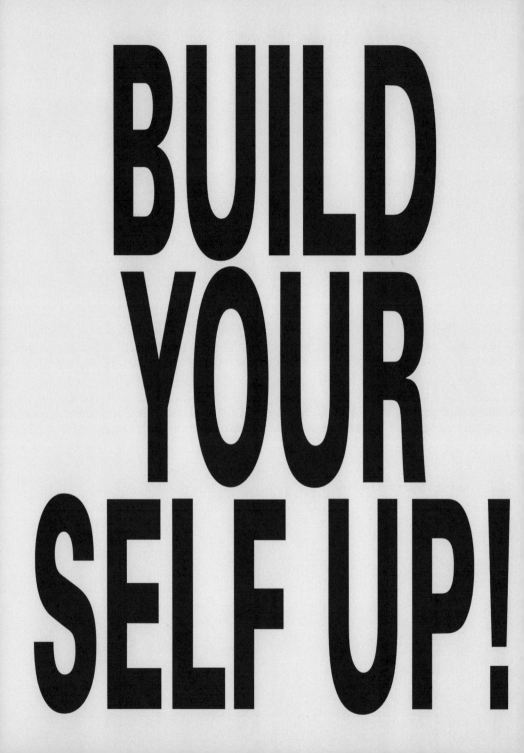

# I love an easy win. Don't you?

An easy win is a small but manageable goal that you completely crush. (I'm thinking of things like arriving ten minutes early to a meeting or packing a healthy lunch or not pushing off important emails until the end of the day.)

Knocking out a bunch of easy wins can make you feel confident and in control.

**Which ones can you rack up?**

- _____
- _____
- _____
- _____
- _____
- _____
- _____
- _____
- _____
- _____

Think back to the
busiest time in
your life—a period
when you truly felt
stretched to your
limits. What were
you balancing?

**Write down a few words
for each obligation here**
(for example: Q3 work
project, four midterms in
one week, or caring for an
ill family member).

Now, how did you manage it
all? Remember the solutions
that helped you. **Are you
able to repurpose them for
this phase in your life?**

# Your name has just been called. Everyone around you is jumping up and down in full celebration mode. You're being whisked onstage.

Now you're standing in front of your peers and your idols, accepting the highest award in the land.

You blink against the lights. Your mouth opens. **What will you say?**

Keep

Going-

CHAPTER 03
# Overcoming Setbacks

## Why did you stop?

Everything was going great. You were moving forward. You were feeling optimistic. And then . . . the inevitable and unavoidable happened. A rejection. A roadblock. An awful day, week, or month. It's so easy to get knocked off your path, no matter how clearly defined it seemed earlier. During these pain points it's tempting to hit pause or even think about quitting altogether.

*Who would know?*

*Who would care?*

*What's the point?*

But you would know. You would care. And the point is finishing what you started. I promise that these frustrating setbacks can actually be stepping stones and opportunities to break new ground. Seriously. You can transform these moments of crisis into a rich foundation for new ideas—and reach the next level in your process. Because you're not a person who is content with standing still, and you're not about to move backward, right? So let's figure out how to move forward once again.

Old ways won't open new doors

**MON:**

_____

_____

**TUE:**

_____

_____

**WED:**

_____

_____

**THU:**

_____

_____

**FRI:**

_____

_____

**SAT:**

_____

_____

**SUN:**

_____

_____

## Routines are good. Ruts are not. How can you switch up your morning routine today?

You don't have to upend _everything_—simply taking a different route, eating an out-of-the-ordinary breakfast, or listening to a new podcast can give you a fresh perspective.

**List some ways you can shake up your schedule and try one out every day this week. Check back in and share how each one made you feel.**

# What is the most outlandish, uncharacteristic thing you could ever do?

Something that would make your closest friend say, "Who are you?!"

**And what is one reward you would receive if you actually did it?**

FORTUNE
FAVORS
THE BOLD

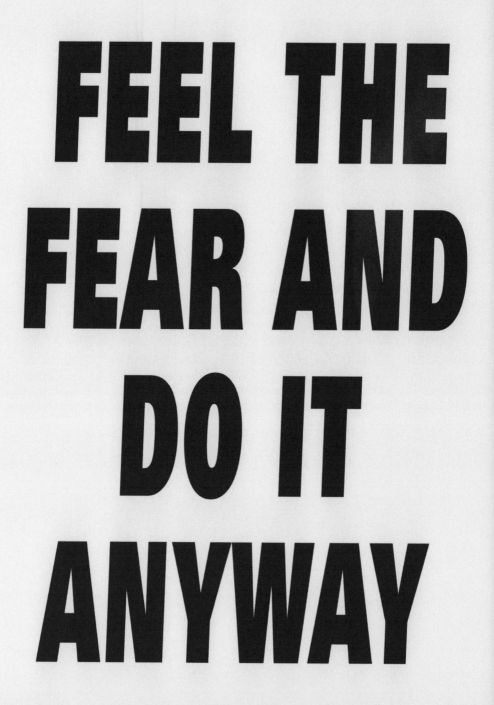

# Have you been procrastinating doing something for months?

**Articulate your biggest fear connected to that thing.** Is it fear of failure, fear of success, fear of feeling dumb, fear of not finishing? Some other kind of fear?

Do you think that fear is valid? Why or why not?

Finally, do that thing. Right now. *Go.*

# Changing your mind-set starts by changing your environment.

Small tweaks make a big difference: lighting a candle, buying a plant, moving around furniture, or hanging a motivational message where you can see it often.

**Do any of your physical spaces feel stagnant? How can you improve them ever so slightly?**

# Reflect on the last rejection you received, whether it was personal or work related.

How did it make you feel? Angry? Defeated? Emboldened? Did it contain any elements of truth?

Sometimes making progress is a numbers game—you have to try, try, try again. **What is one way you can try again?**

*Pssst.* Nobody
is watching you.
I know that seems
hard to believe,
but it's true.

If you're late releasing your
project into the world, or feel
like you've screwed up, I'm
here to tell you . . . people
aren't paying that much
attention. Nobody's clocking
your failures.

**Now that we're on the
same page, what's one
activity you can do to move
forward—and move on—
right now?**

When failure happens, it's natural to want to take it out with yesterday's trash and move on as quickly as possible.

But let's sit with it for a minute. **What is one failure you experienced lately? Ask yourself: What lesson is this trying to teach me?** Do you need to prepare more, or seek out help?

Now when you think of your failure, you can reflect on everything you've learned instead of everything you've lost.

# What did you want to be when you grew up?

**Pinpoint two key moments in your early life that defined the career you have today.**

1. _____

   _____

   _____

   _____

   _____

   _____

2. _____

   _____

   _____

   _____

   _____

   _____

If you're feeling overwhelmed, you need time and space to think. The only way to find it? Say no.

Say no to invitations that feel like obligations. Say no to voluntary tasks that feel like chores. Say no to being busy and say yes to freedom.

Because once you say no, you don't ever have to think about that decision again. **What will you say no to today?**

X _____

X _____

X _____

X _____

X _____

X _____

X _____

X _____

X _____

X _____

The way you speak to yourself matters

# What story are you telling yourself right now?

Are you saying, "I'm not good enough or smart enough" or, "Everyone's already so far ahead of me"?

What if I told you those things weren't true? What if I said you are good enough, and smart enough, and you're not running the same race as anybody else?

**How would you change your story if you knew that someone out there believed in you?**

# The opposite of *force* is *allow*.

Instead of forcing your project into existence, how can you give permission to your work instead?

**Finish this sentence:**

**Today, I will allow my work to** _____

_____

_____

_____

_____

_____

_____

_____

_____

_____

# Have you tried Googling it?

It might sound silly, but sometimes our process stalls when we literally don't know how to complete the next step. Take advantage of all the knowledge surrounding you.

**Create a list of five "how do I?" questions you can look up today—and then find the answers.**

**How do I**

?

**How do I**

?

**How do I**

?

**How do I**

?

**How do I**

?

# Need more energy? Try a caffeine nap.

It's simple—when you're tired, drink a cup of coffee, then immediately lie down and set a timer for twenty minutes. When the timer goes off, you'll wake up refreshed (that's the caffeine kicking in).

But here's a twist: Before you sleep, think of one problem you're going to tackle when you wake up. **Write that problem down here and come back when you have the solution.**

**Problem:**

_____

_____

_____

_____

_____

_____

**Solution:**

_____

_____

_____

_____

_____

_____

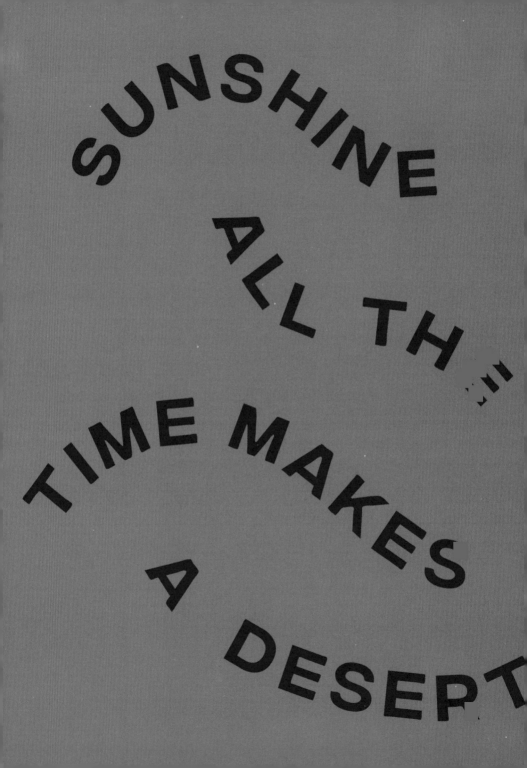

# Nothing is perfect.

But when life gives you a downpour, rather than pretending it's seventy-two degrees and sunny, sometimes it's better to hunker down and wait out the storm.

**What's the reality of your current storm? When do you believe it will pass?**

Imagine that every
goal you have
isn't *impossible*,
but *inevitable*.

Finishing is inevitable.
Success is inevitable.
Rising above is inevitable.

**What does inevitability
feel like to you?**

WHAT IF EVERY
THING YOU'RE GOING
THROUGH IS
PREPARING YOU
FOR WHAT YOU
ASKED FOR

# CHAPTER 04

# Following Through

**Are you ready?**

You're creating. You're doing the work.
You're jumping over hurdles. The end is in sight.
If you're hitting the brakes, ask yourself: Why?

It's time to push past resistance and go where
you've never been.

Now is the time to take the next step—to share
your work, find a champion, and propel your
project up, up, and away. The most brilliant ideas
in the world aren't worth anything if they remain
ideas in your head. You must expose them to the
outside world, invite collaborators or an audience,
and allow your dreams to evolve into what they
always wanted to be. You must make them
unmistakably real.

This is the rare and vital (and yes, somewhat
stressful) moment of *crossing the finish line*. You're
going to harness the emotional and physical energy
necessary to hit your deadlines and see your
project through. You're going to let it soar, all on
its own.

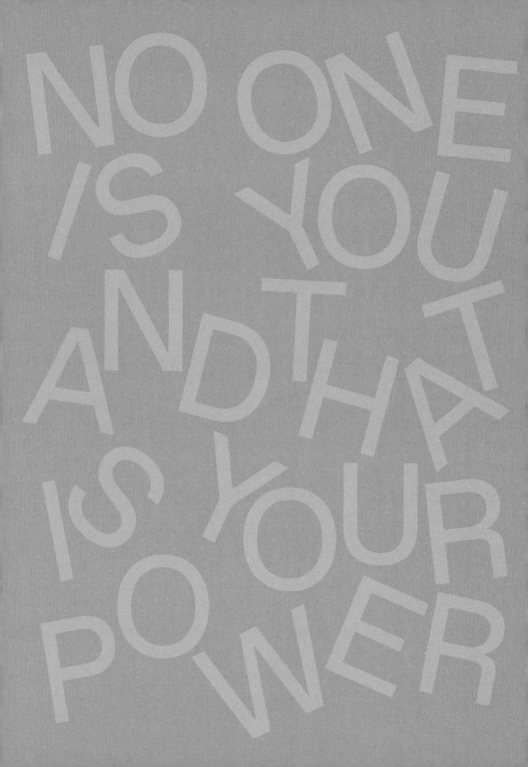

## Whatever hurdle you're facing, you've probably faced a variation of it before.

How did you push past it? By asking for help? Reframing your goal? Working for five solid hours?

Whatever you did then, that is your superpower—and you can use it again and again.

**Name your superpower here.**

I want you to imagine your future self.

The one who has everything figured out (or most of it, anyway). The one who's achieved the goals you set at the beginning of this journey. Your future self is happy, confident, satisfied.

**Now imagine what advice your future self would give you in this moment. Slow down? Speed up? Work more, or less? What is your future self telling you?**

# Surrounding yourself with the right people can take your ideas to the next level.

What was the most exciting room you were recently in? Which conversation do you remember the most? That person could be one of the right people for you.

**Reach out today** and ask what they're working on—and if there's a way you can support what they're doing.

Rituals can help you focus not only because they're calming, but because they condition you to know instantly what you're supposed to be doing next.

Some people brew a cup of tea or do stretches to get in the zone. Others need a bit of sunshine or to scroll through social media. (I'm partial to chewing sunflower seeds.)

**Explain the rituals that are most important to you.**

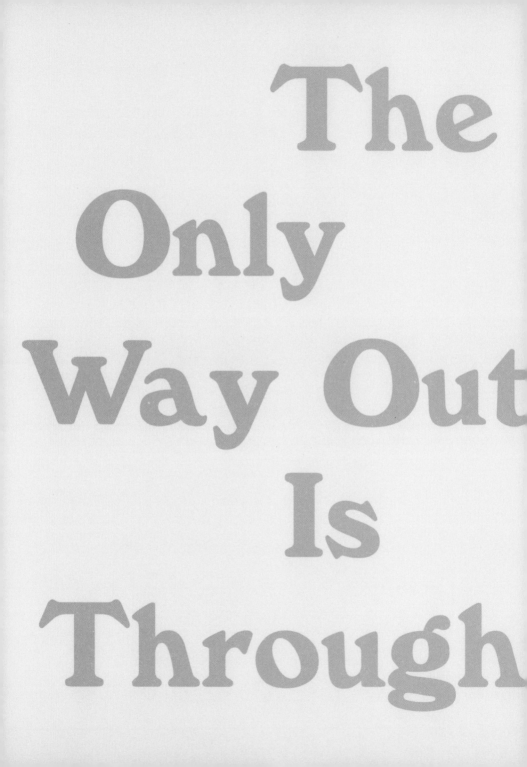

Take this journal for a walk (even if it's only to the other room).

Go to the coziest space you can find. Write down everything you hear, from snippets of conversation to birds chirping.

**Do these sounds hold any clues for your current project?**

- _____
- _____
- _____
- _____
- _____
- _____
- _____
- _____
- _____
- _____

Your goal today is to ship something you've been thinking about for a while. This means finishing *anything* and sending it off to someone else.

You've already committed a lot of time to not doing it. (Probably more time than it would take to actually finish it.)

**So, what will you ship once and for all and get off your mind forever?**

By letting go, it all gets done.

Forward momentum will push you into new territories.

Today, start a one-task streak. Commit to one small action a day for the next seven days. Make one call, write one paragraph, apply to one job, whatever you need.

**What streak will you start? Mark a big X on this page for every day you keep it up.**

**Task:**

_____

_____

**Day 1** ☐

**Day 2** ☐

**Day 3** ☐

**Day 4** ☐

**Day 5** ☐

**Day 6** ☐

**Day 7** ☐

# What is one song that makes you feel completely you?

**Write the title and as many of the lyrics as you can remember here.**

Then go put it on and get ready to receive everything you deserve.

What you love,

you empower.

What you fear,

you empower.

What you empower,

you attract.

What do you love today?

What do you fear today?

What are you going to attract today?

**I love**

_____

_____

_____

**I fear**

_____

_____

_____

**I will attract**

_____

_____

_____

# Are you in a situation where you feel like you're settling for the bare minimum?

Sometimes to get to the next level we need to raise the stakes. You know how: You have to do something that makes you a little nervous.

**How can you raise the stakes?**

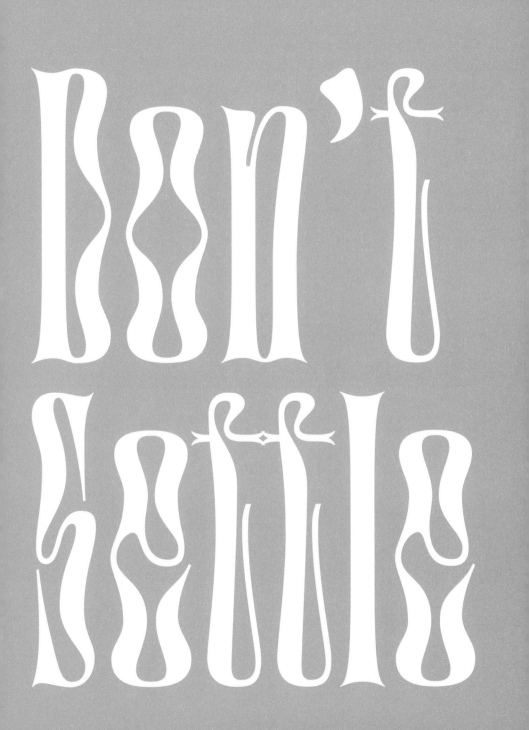

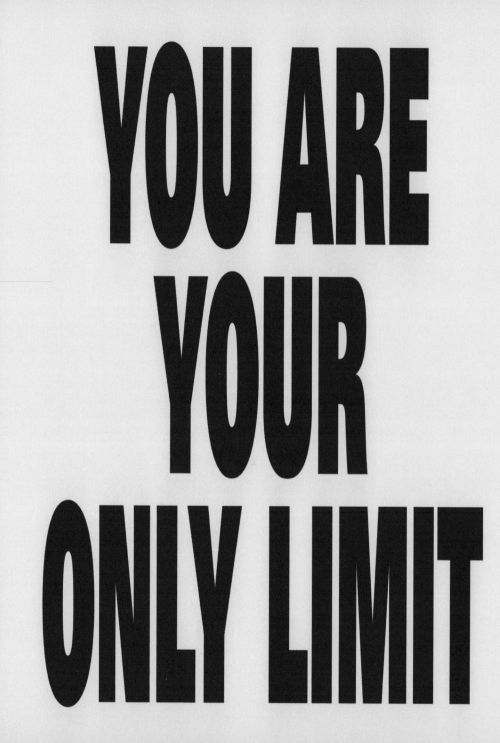

What is the biggest limiting factor in your life right now? Do you need more time, energy, inspiration, money? (Or all of 'em?)

What if I told you that each of those limiting factors was in your ability to control? That you have complete power over your thoughts and your actions.

**What is one way you can push past a limit today?**

When you board
a plane, the pilot
shares the ETA
(estimated time
of arrival) for
your destination.
Let's steal this.

**What's your ETA for the next
phase of your project?**

Remember: This is an
estimate. Sometimes you'll
fly faster or slower—and
that's OK.

# Some—times, later be—comes never

# You've been transported to a remote island and are cut off from all your obligations back home.

You have complete freedom, all the tools you need, unlimited caffeine—and no Internet to distract you.

**What will you work on?**

Now pick a time to turn your phone to airplane mode and pretend you're on the island.

# Can you imagine giving up on your project and handing it over to someone else?

Or does the thought of that make you wince and want to grab hold of it even tighter?

**Explain why you are the only person who can put the finishing touches on this idea.**

# Take me back in time.

Can you recall the first
moment you said yes to
your project?

**Why did you say yes?**
**Describe the reasons here.**

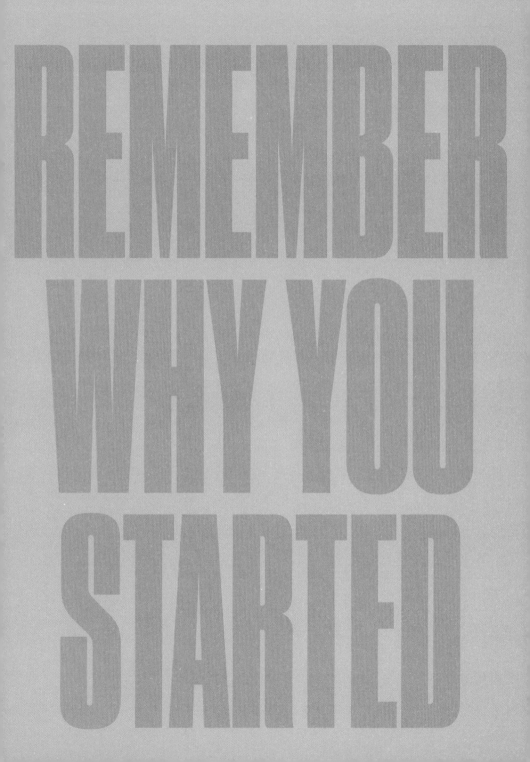

**CHAPTER 05**

# Seeking Closure

**How does finishing feel?**

The anxiety of starting is over. The thrill of being immersed in the moment has passed. The angst of solving problems is long gone. You've done all that you can do. Your project finally feels done.

But your journey isn't over.

Carving out time to celebrate, reflect, and maybe even plot the future is equally as important as every step you took to reach the end. While it feels rewarding to achieve a goal, this macro accomplishment can create a whirlwind that drowns out all the micro steps you took toward the finish line. You might even find yourself asking: *How did this happen?*

You can discover lessons along the way by analyzing your process and looking backward. With this after-the-fact perspective, you can ask yourself what went wrong, what went right, and what you'll do differently the next time. Because there will be a next time, and it's just around the corner.

EVERY NEXT
LEVEL OF
YOUR LIFE WILL
DEMAND A
DIFFERENT
VERSION OF YOU

## Consider your
## recent project . . .

What is the main emotion you felt at the beginning?

And how do you feel now, nearing the end?

**List three skills you sharpened over that time.** Maybe you became more disciplined, a better collaborator, or more receptive to feedback.

1. _____

_____

_____

2. _____

_____

_____

3. _____

_____

_____

You've done an amazing job. You deserve every gold star. You can bask in the glory. But— *but*—I also want to challenge you to go a little further.

There's a good chance there is one more step you can take. One more person to contact. One more avenue to explore. One more push to make.

**Figure out what that extra step is here. Even if it seems out of reach or unlikely, try to put it into words.**

I didn't come this far to only come this far

# Sometimes it's hard to see how far you've come.

Think about a year ago. Where exactly were you? How did you spend your days? Who were you with?

**Write down everything you can recall from that time.**

# You've just been given a thousand dollars. (Yay!)

The only rule is that you have to spend all of it on celebrating yourself and your project.

**What would you do with the money?**

# GRATITUDE IS HEAVEN ITSELF

# Let's talk gratitude.

Showing appreciation for your process isn't always easy, but it's necessary.

**What is one part of your process that often trips you up, but that you're always grateful for?**

Leaving a city.
Typing "The end."
Closing a business
deal. These final
moments can give
you a sense of
completion and
satisfaction.

Take a moment to consider
your next project, even if it's
only a dream right now.

**What do you want that
ending to feel like?**

I AM
COMPLETE
BUT I'M NOT
FINISHED

Consider your evening routine. List everything you do between dinner and your head hitting the pillow.

Put a star by the activities that relax you (perhaps reading or talking to a loved one). Make a checkmark by the activities that stress you out (taking one last peek at email).

**Finally, circle the activities you're going to do tonight.**

**Activities:**

☐ _____

☐ _____

☐ _____

☐ _____

☐ _____

☐ _____

☐ _____

☐ _____

☐ _____

☐ _____

Think about
your all-time
favorite book.

Remember how each chapter unfolded and inched toward the end. Every page was essential to move on to the next.

**If your life was a book, which chapter are you in right now? Give your book a title and write the opening paragraph.**

EVERY
DAY IN
EVERY
WAY, I'M
GETTING
BETTER
AND
BETTER

Getting even
just one percent
better every
day at a task or
behavior can lead
to extraordinary
changes.

**What is one habit you could
put an extra one percent of
effort into today?**

## Are you *completely* done?

To make sure your mind is free, I'd like to introduce the essential practice I call "Clear the Decks," which scrubs away any nagging, leftover tasks related to your project, so you can truly turn to the next chapter.

**Your mission is to clear your own decks. What are your last to-dos?**

- _____

- _____

- _____

- _____

- _____

- _____

- _____

- _____

- _____

# The best way to absorb a lesson is to teach it to someone else.

Think about the process you've gone through. Is there anyone you know who could benefit from hearing your story?

**How can you pay forward what you've learned? Write the biggest lesson here and decide who you're going to share it with.**

# Let's say you will be granted one wish for a future project.

You can receive one of the following: ten times more money, ten times more time, or ten times more praise.

**Which one would you choose? More time, money, or praise? Why?**

'Time² or money³ or Praise'

# If you had to start your process all over again, what could you definitely live without?

**Be as specific as possible about what you would do differently.**

# Letting go makes room for future opportunities.

Share what you want to let go of—and what you think is coming.

**What is gone:**

_____

_____

_____

_____

_____

_____

**What is coming:**

_____

_____

_____

_____

_____

_____

Finally, after everything you've been through, everything you've shared and uncovered and accomplished, I have only one question for you:

## What's next?

Editor: Madeline Jaffe
Designer: Diane Shaw
Production Manager: Rebecca Westall

ISBN: 978-1-4197-4346-7
Text © 2020 Kara Cutruzzula
Illustrations © 2020 Tessa Forrest
Cover © 2020 Abrams

Printed and bound in China
10 9 8

Abrams Image products are available at special discounts
when purchased in quantity for premiums and promotions
as well as fundraising or educational use. Special editions
can also be created to specification. For details, contact
specialsales@abramsbooks.com or the address below.

Abrams Image® is a registered trademark of Harry N. Abrams, Inc.

**ABRAMS** The Art of Books
195 Broadway, New York, NY 10007
abramsbooks.com

MIX
Paper from
responsible sources
FSC
www.fsc.org
FSC™ C144853